DREAM JOBS IN SPORTS MARKETING

HEATHER MOORE NIVER

ROSEN
PUBLISHING®

New York

Published in 2013 by The Rosen Publishing Group, Inc.
29 East 21st Street, New York, NY 10010

Copyright © 2013 by The Rosen Publishing Group, Inc.

First Edition

Library of Congress Cataloging-in-Publication Data

Niver, Heather Moore.
Dream jobs in sports marketing/Heather Moore Niver.
    p. cm.—(Great careers in the sports industry)
Includes bibliographical references and index.
ISBN 978-1-4488-6900-8 (library binding)
1. Sports—Marketing. 2. Sports—Vocational guidance. I. Title.
GV716.N58 2012
796.0688—dc23

                                                    2011040669

Manufactured in the United States of America

CPSIA Compliance Information: Batch #S12YA: For further information, contact Rosen Publishing, New York, New

York, at 1-800-237-9932.

CONTENTS

INTRODUCTION

Billboards and signs are a great way to market products at games and support teams like the Portland Sea Dogs at Hadlock field in Portland, Maine.

After months of planning, working out strategies, and e-mail blitzes to the team's fans, opening day for the city's new ballpark is finally here. The local baseball team is here for the opening game against its longstanding rivals. Seats have been sold out for weeks. Bright flags and banners have been advertising the event around the city and surrounding towns for weeks. Today they flap in the breeze in front of the park to greet the crowds as they arrive.

Robyn Tanner has been the marketing manager for the event since day one, and she has worked some long hours to make sure everything will run smoothly and on time. Just yesterday, baseball hats featuring the team's logo arrived in time to give to the first five hundred entrants. Tanner's promotions manager had ordered them more than a month ago, but their order was held up when an editor in the creative department caught a spelling error in the text. When the shipping company delivered the boxes late yesterday afternoon, everyone in the marketing department breathed a huge sigh of relief. Student interns from the nearby university and the high school greet the spectators and hand out the colored hats, and Tanner smiles to see so may little kids wearing them in the stands already.

As people enter the park, smiling workers wearing team staff T-shirts offer samples of ice cream to entice customers to buy more of the local dairy's frozen desserts.

It's a hot Saturday afternoon, and Tanner is pleased to see that many people head straight for the ice cream booth just behind the students. A percentage of today's profits, from the ice cream sales and other drinks and snacks at the concession stand, will be donated to the city's hospital. Tanner made sure to include this detail on all the advertisements and knows that it encouraged more people to come out on a busy summer Saturday with so many other fun things to do in and around the city. The donations associate the new baseball park with the hospital and show the public that although the park is about fun, it also cares about community health.

Other local businesses are supporting the park, too, so Tanner's marketing team included all their logos in the large banners around town. They are also shown on both the free baseball hats and backs of the orange staff T-shirts.

Earlier in the day, Tanner's marketing team sent out one last blast of e-mails and microblogging posts to remind fans of the game and game day promotions. They had the event posted on their social media pages months before and had been updating fans on the event's progress and special features like pre-game performances by local musicians.

The spectators are taking their seats. The stands are almost full. The players run out onto the field and the crowd leaps to its feet. The cheers echo through the park. It's time to play ball!

People have been playing sports since we first walked the earth. Homer's *Iliad* might be the first written account of sports in literature, according to Stedman Graham, Lisa Delpy Meirotti, and Joe Jeff Goldblatt, authors of *The Ultimate Guide to Sports Marketing*, proving that people have been competing in athletics for a long time. John P. Bevilaqua, author of *What Exactly Is Sports Marketing?*, defines sports marketing as creating a setting for a sale. Marketing comes in when a sale is for a specific type of goods, like sports. Sports marketers want their products and events to stand out above all others.

Sports marketing goes back over a hundred years when tobacco companies made what may be the first baseball cards. Cards showing pictures of baseball players were put into cigarette boxes to increase sales and encourage buyers to purchase their brand. This may have been the first sports promotion. It soon burst into the bubble gum industry, and bubble gum baseball cards have been collected by baseball fans of all ages ever since. The cards don't even have bubble gum in them anymore, but baseball cards are still popular. Likewise, sports marketing continues to exist and thrive today.

Chapter 1
THE INS AND OUTS OF SPORTS MARKETING

In general, the idea of marketing sports seems like it should be cut and dry. Sports marketing sounds like simply encouraging consumers to buy a product. But as the popularity of sports skyrockets and the money spent on sports soars, marketing is anything but simple.

Marketing is sometimes divided into two smaller parts: macromarketing and micromarketing. Generally, macromarketing is the course that guides goods and services from the producer to the consumer. In other words, this is the process that moves soccer balls from the company that makes them to the athletes that buy them. Micromarketing is a part of the macromarketing system. It is the actions of each provider of goods and services. This includes the e-mail blasts, the promotions, and the banners that a company's marketers create to get its product noticed and purchased. In the case of marketing in sports, the goods include more than just physical items like snowboards and team jerseys.

Modern marketing, whether it is for football or rock music, has become more complex over the years. Marketing includes planning and developing products (new and existing), organizing how the product will reach the customer, wholesaling, setting the prices, advertising and promotion, and public relations, to name just a few parts of it. Ken Kaser and Dotty B. Oelkers, coauthors of *Sports and Entertainment Marketing*, list seven major tasks for marketing sports (or anything else): "marketing-information management, product/service management, finance, price, promotion, selling, and distribution."

MARKETING OF SPORTS AND MARKETING THROUGH SPORTS

Sports marketing has two basic angles: the marketing of sports and the marketing through sports. Marketing of sports is pretty simple. It often involves advertising sports (such as tennis or skateboarding) and sports associations (such as the National Football Association). Basically, marketing of sports advertises and promotes sports as a whole. Marketing through sports means using sports or a sports figure to promote a product.

The marketed product does not have to be sports related. In 1921 Jockey underwear was endorsed by Babe Ruth. In 2011, skateboarder Clint Peterson rolled his way through a television commercial for Stride chewing gum

The Target corporation is not a sports organization, but it used symbols and popular Olympian snowboarder Shaun White in New York City's Times Square to market its stores.

on his board. The commercial even included an appearance by snowboard Olympian Shaun White.

EAT YOUR WHEATIES

Wheaties is a classic example of marketing through sports. Breakfast cereal does not have a whole lot to do with sports. But almost everyone recognizes the bright orange box of Wheaties cereal with an athlete on the front. General Mills started putting athletes like Lou Gehrig on the backs of their cereal boxes in the 1930s. In 1984, Olympic gymnast Mary Lou Retton became the first woman to be on a box of Wheaties. Soon every athlete hoped to grace the cover of a Wheaties box. Sports stars from baseball, swimming, skiing, golf, and even NASCAR (National Association for Stock Car Auto Racing) have been on the box.

In 2009, Wheaties partnered with athletes and nutritionists to do some marketing of sports. Wheaties FUEL is a high-energy, high-fiber cereal developed specifically for athletes. Its slogan is "By Champions. For Champions." In one marketing campaign FUEL teamed up with Clint Bowyer and the No. 33 Richard Childress Racing team. A flashy black and orange Chevrolet race car displayed the Wheaties FUEL logo. Wheaties FUEL is the official sponsor of Ironman, a 140.6-mile

A box of high-fiber, high-energy Wheaties FUEL cereal features baseball player Albert Pujols to promote the brand.

(226.2 km) race that involves 2.4 miles (3.8 km) of swimming, 112 miles (180.2 km) of bike riding, and 26.2 miles (42.1 km) of running. Those athletes certainly would need their Wheaties to power through all those miles.

THE ENDORSERS

Who are the sports figures and celebrities advertising these products? Of course athletes make up a large percentage of endorsements, whether they are famous medal and trophy winners who make the national news or local and amateur athletes. Sports celebrities consist of coaches, the team's owners, sports officials, and even sports media members.

CAREERS IN SPORTS MARKETING

There are lots of career options, but be interested in the career no matter what is being marketed. Students

BE YOUR OWN BOSS

Lots of young job seekers start out by looking for a job with a company. They may start out at the ground floor and work their way up or jump right into things closer to the top. But after many years with the same company or even after trying out a few companies, some people want to take their years of experience and be their own boss. These are entrepreneurs. Ben Sturner, founder of Leverage Agency, is one such entrepreneur, reports Robert Tuchman for *Entrepreneur* magazine.

Sturner started out trying some sports marketing and event management internships, then later landed a job with a company. Eventually, he decided to go out on his own. Sturner began by working out of his apartment and had only one client. He eventually increased his client base to more than thirty and now offers "sponsorship packaging, strategy and sales, content distribution,... public relations communications, corporate consulting, creative web design, and social media marketing." An entrepreneur gets to be the boss, which can be a huge draw for some people. But if the business expands, the entrepreneur may have to hire employees, which is an added responsibility. Entrepreneurs often work late nights and weekends, too.

should choose their area of study based on the basic career. Whether the job is marketing peanut butter or polo, be interested in the marketing itself. This strategy trans-

WINNING WITH SOCIAL NETWORKING

Social networking Web sites are all the rage with everyone from teenagers to businesses. "Athletes are focusing on growing their fan bases," says sports agent Darren Heitner. Athletes, agents, and all kinds of sports businesses use sites such as Twitter. Sports promoter and Ultimate Fighting Championship (UFC) president Dana White updates his Facebook page with posts from Twitter (called "tweets"). Others use Facebook and Google+ to gain followers and follow other people and businesses in the industry. These social sites can be a good marketing tool. People who follow an athlete or company on one of these networks learn about upcoming events and games, for example. These sites are a great way to learn about others in the field and what they are doing, making them good for networking, too.

These networks are a great chance to start sports conversations and keep the followers engaged. There is nothing wrong with being friendly and even funny on these sites, but it is important to keep the message positive and fairly professional.

lates into more job opportunities in the long run, but most of all it helps a student choose a career that should be interesting and satisfying. One of the beauties of the sports marketing world is the number and variety of careers available.

BUYERS AND SPONSORS

As the name suggests, buyers (also known as purchasing managers and purchasing agents) are in charge of buying products for their companies. Buyers want to get the best products for the best deal, which usually means the lowest price. Sponsors associate with a team or event by giving them money to put on the event or support the team. The sponsor gets advertising around the country or even the world as the company name is included with nearly every mention of the event, on television, on the radio, on the Internet, and in print.

PROMOTERS

Sports promoters and demonstrators get consumers excited about buying sports products and attending sporting events. Promoters of athletes, like the recognizable Don King, might do many things, such as create the event, advertise it, and make sure everything is legal and all contracts are signed. For products, a promoter might actually have samples of the product at stores, shopping malls, or stadiums to entice consumers and stores to buy it. Sometimes they take the names and contact information of people who might be interested so they can add them to mailing and e-mail lists.

PUBLIC RELATIONS

Public relations jobs involve making sure the team, athlete, product, or event has a good reputation. Sometimes this means emphasizing good deeds, such as charity work or donations. Other times it means smoothing over a bad story or explaining a company's point of view. Public relations managers keep an eye on different trends that might concern the team or athlete and make suggestions about what they should do.

BROADCASTING

Broadcasters and announcers certainly get a lot of airtime on television and radio. They sometimes have the memorable voices and personalities that call the plays that put the audience on the edge of its seat. But most marketing jobs in the field of broadcasting are not in front of the camera or microphone. Broadcasting managers and sales are just a couple of the professions behind the scenes that put the anchors on the air to broadcast the games, athletes, and sports news to eager viewers and listeners.

SPORTS FACILITY AND VENUE MARKETING

Facilities and venues host and stage events. There are plenty of job opportunities in sports marketing at a

Announcers Curt Menefee (*left*) and Terry Bradshaw discuss the football game, its plays, and the key players during halftime to keep the audience engaged and interested until the game resumes.

sports venue from the amateur to the professional level. Golf courses, fitness centers, and race tracks are all under sports venues as well. Many aspects of these facilities need promotion and marketing to draw in the customers and fill the stadium seats or join their health clubs.

SPORT EVENTS MANAGEMENT AND OPERATIONS

Sport events management and operations generally involves marketing everything that happens during the event, such as selling tickets, team merchandise, and food and beverages. All these things help the event make a profit and get people enthusiastic about the event. The event can include regular team games throughout a sports season or a week-long event that happens only every few years, such as the Olympics.

Chapter 2

HIGH SCHOOL AND COLLEGE YEARS

The years during high school and college are an excellent time to start researching sports marketing programs and deciding whether it is the right career choice. Trying out the many different careers in sports marketing is one of the best ways to make a decision. Students don't have to commit to a career now, so this is the time to try new things. At this stage of the game, there is always the option to go in another direction. This is the time to move on to something else if it doesn't seem like a good fit. If it seems really interesting, dive deeper into the details of that career and learn all about it.

NETWORKING

Networking is a useful way to meet new people in the sports marketing industry to get information, internships, and jobs. Employers are often more enthusiastic

Networking is key to a successful sports marketing career. Even writing a simple e-mail can be an effective way to meet people who are already in the sports marketing field.

about hiring an employee who comes with a good reference from someone they know. Sometimes it can help to get in touch with someone in the business even without a direct connection through a friend or colleague. This is sometimes called cold calling.

Sima Dahl, a marketing consultant, sales trainer, and keynote speaker, outlines several simple tips, or "rules of engagement" for the American Marketing Association that might help get a foot in the door—or at least prevent getting the door slammed shut before making a request. First, a job seeker should do some research and know some general information about the company or individual he or she is targeting. Sometimes this can be as easy as a quick Internet search to get some basic details, which can also help avoid asking for facts that are readily available online or in publications. Professionalism and good manners are always welcome and make a good impression. Pleas for help, however, may come across as desperate, having the opposite effect. Commenting about a recent Twitter, Facebook, or Google+ post suggests the letter writer has done his or her research and is keeping up with what's going on. Finally, a simple thank you is always a good way to go. Making sure the request to the contact is reasonable or has a flexible timeframe makes it easier for the person, who is likely busy, to help out.

NETWORKING: IT'S ALL ABOUT WHOM YOU KNOW

It's no joke when people say that getting a job is based on whom you know. Prospects may seem dismal when the job goal is marketing for the Olympics or the X Games, but in fact some simple networking steps can yield surprisingly effective and far-reaching results. Atlanta Braves director of ticket operations Anthony Esposito got his first job with a professional sports organization thanks to some networking with the Charlotte Knights, a AAA baseball team. A fellow sports management major at his college recommended him for an internship with the team, and he landed an intern position in the ticket office with the Knights. "I split my time between working in the Ticket Office and being the catcher in the bullpen during games. Great experience! When my internship was over I kept in touch with my bosses at the Knights and helped out at the ballpark whenever I had time between school and baseball games. I was hired on full time prior to my graduation ... That is where it all began."

It's hard to say what contacts might come in handy when looking for a new job, so it's a good idea to keep in touch with coworkers, teachers, and former employers.

SCORING AN INTERNSHIP

An internship is a great way to test out a job. It provides on-the-job experience and exposes the good, the bad, and the ugly parts of the job. An internship can teach a student about the world of employment and what it's like to work for a boss, go to meetings, and meet deadlines. Of course, internships are a great way to meet people already in the business of sports marketing. They might be good connections for networking when an official job search begins.

WHAT AN INTERNSHIP INVOLVES

Most internships are geared toward college students, but some are suitable for high school students or even adults looking to make a career change. Some high schools offer to help arrange internships, and other times the company helps get the ball rolling. Some internships offer a paycheck for the work, others offer school credit, and some come with both. The sporting goods company Nike offers internships in sports marketing that include not only a paycheck but use of their athletic facilities and an employee discount at their employee stores, among other perks. With such a sweet deal, it's no wonder the competition to score Nike internships is tough. Many students try to get a summer internship after their junior year of

Job fairs are another way to learn about internships with marketing firms and sports venues. Job recruiters also attend job fairs, so it's a good idea to bring a résumé and contact information.

college, but it is certainly possible to intern during the school year. Some internships last longer than a single semester.

WHERE INTERNSHIPS ARE LOCATED

Internships may be located just about anywhere in the world. To find out where there might be openings for an internship, do some research at public libraries, career centers, school counseling offices, and college resource centers. Some newspapers and online job listings also advertise internships. Check out job fairs, too. College advisers and professors might have suggestions or know of opportunities. They may also be able to suggest good internships that other sports marketing students have enjoyed. Be sure to ask friends and family for ideas, especially if they have any connections with marketing or, better yet, sports marketing.

SCOUTING OUT AN INTERNSHIP

Ideally, the internship will focus on a particular branch of sports marketing that the student finds interesting. However, a general marketing job in another field will offer just as useful an experience, even if it is not specifically related to sports. Interning with the marketing manager of a music distributor will be just as useful as interning with the marketing manager for a sporting goods manufacturer. Remember to focus on the basic job, whether it is associated with sports or not. To combine a satisfying job with an enjoyable sport is just a bonus.

INTERNSHIP WARM-UP

Some preparation for internship applications is always a good idea. Marketing internships can be a challenge, simply because so many students want them. For example, the Nike Web site explains, "It takes more than just a passion for sport to stay on top of our game. That's why at Nike we seek the exceptional, the motivated and the innovative. Our highly competitive internship programs provide candidates with the opportunity to gain the best hands-on experience in virtually every area within Nike." Also consider writing up a résumé and cover letter. A résumé is a chance to outline your experience and background in a way that is easy to skim. The cover letter is an opportunity to go into detail or give the would-be employer information that does not come across in the résumé. A cover letter is a good place for details about past experience, such as advertisements and marketing for the high school pep rally that packed the stands.

WHY INTERNSHIPS ARE WORTH IT

Not sure an internship is worth the legwork it will take to find one? Elka Jones offers some eye-opening statistics that might change some opinions: "According to a 2005 survey by the National Association of Colleges and Employers, employers reported that, on average, more than 3 out of 5 college hires had internship experience. Moreover, many employers hire directly from their internship programs. The association's survey also reported that, on average, more than half of all students were offered a full-time job after completing their internship." It may be tempting to spend all summer at the beach playing volleyball, but clearly putting some time in at an internship can score some points, too.

A FOOT IN THE DOOR

Once an internship interview is offered, make the most of it. The College Board suggests asking a lot of questions. Don't be shy. Find out the job's duties, and ask to speak with the supervisor who will be in charge of the internship. Talking to other interns is a good move, too. They can share all the dirt about what it is like to work at that company, and they have a different perspective from the employer or supervisors.

Don't forget that at an internship interview, questions are just as important as a professional résumé. Feel free to ask about the job and what the company expects of its interns.

ACING THE INTERVIEW

Not sure about wowing that Nike marketing executive in an interview? Try some practice or "mock" interviews to get the feel of how an interview might go. This may lessen any nervousness. And it helps the job seeker know what kinds of questions to expect. Career centers offer opportunities to try rehearsal interviews. Even a friend or family member can help stage a mock interview.

IN COLLEGE

If college seems like a good step after high school, go for it. Not all jobs require a degree, but more and more employers do look for a bachelor's degree. There are plenty of eye-catching careers in sports marketing but be sure that the basics of the course of study are interesting, whether

More and more employers are looking for candidates with a bachelor's degree. If college is part of the game plan, consider a degree and classes in marketing or business.

they involve sports or not. Some general degrees to consider are marketing and business. Some employers look for a background in kinesiology, too, which is the study of how the human body moves.

Former vice president of marketing for the Women's National Basketball Association (WNBA) Stephanie Hofmann advises that a philosophy of "more breadth than depth" is a good way to go. A general degree in marketing will allow the student to use his or her education in any field, which can be handy in an economy where competition for jobs is tight. Also, a general degree allows a person to change gears later on in life if sports marketing no longer seems like a good career. The field of sports can have some wild hours. It might be hard to believe, but as one gets older or starts a family, a regular schedule might be more appealing.

CLASSES AND COURSES

Always research the college or university before signing up for classes. Unfortunately, not all schools are created equal. Be sure that they seem like a good fit, but also make sure the schools are accredited. Some colleges offer online courses that can be taken remotely. These are handy for students who are already employed or prefer to take classes from home.

Whether to go on to graduate school is a big decision. Some degrees take years to achieve, and tuition is expensive, often requiring loans unless scholarships are available. Some people might argue that a master's in business will not result in a better job or a higher salary, but experience will. That said, others feel a higher degree such as a master's or a doctorate gives any job applicant a leg up in a competitive job market. Really, the decision comes down to the individual and whether grad school seems like a good fit, in terms of education, time, and finances. Many graduate classes can be taken at night or online, making it possible to hold a job during the day or take classes at a remote university without relocating.

Chapter 3
SPORTS BUYERS AND SPONSORS

To say that sports is a big-money business is to put it mildly. Take a look at how many television channels and prime-time program slots are dominated by sports coverage. The amount of money that goes into these shows, televised events, and—of course—the commercials and advertisements grows every year. Companies spend millions of dollars on sports, and much of it goes toward marketing.

Buyers and sponsors are usually willing to pay lots of money to advertise on the air, in stadiums/venues, on the radio, and at different events. The Olympics and NASCAR (National Association for Stock Car Auto Racing) are excellent examples of booming commercial entertainment opportunities. One-day events such as the Super Bowl (football), Wimbledon (tennis), and the Kentucky Derby (horse racing) are other big event marketing opportunities.

More and more often, sponsors are paying to have their company name as part of the venue name. For example, the 2010 Sports Facility of the Year award went to Target Field in Minneapolis. Target Field beat out the likes of Pittsburgh's Consol Energy Center and the Red Bull Arena in Harrison, N.J.

OLYMPIC-SIZED MARKETING

Today the Olympic Games are the biggest money-making event in sports. The sheer number of sports programming, sponsorships, and events has flourished, especially since

Coke was a major sponsor of the 2008 Olympic Games in Beijing, China, with Coca-Cola chairman and CEO Neville Isdell (*left*) and International Olympic Committee president Jacques Rogge partnering to market the event.

the 1984 Olympic Games held in Los Angeles, California. That's pretty impressive for some games that started out to honor the Greek god Zeus.

In terms of advertising, the Olympics are one of a kind. These games do not have advertisers; they have sponsors. In turn, sponsors make plenty of money from the games.

SPONSORSHIPS

Sponsorship can actually be quite complex. It's not as simple as just writing a company check, providing a nifty logo, and then sitting back as the profits roll in. Sponsorship involves a lot of risk. Car manufacturer BMW sponsored an America's Cup sailboat called the *Oracle*. When the team did not place in the qualifying race, the *Oracle* was out of the main race before the bow hit the water. As a result, BMW may have lost $200 million.

A big loss like that definitely makes a company take a closer look at whether a sponsorship is a good idea. The would-be sponsor must ask whether the business gained from having its name splashed all over the event or athlete makes up for the potential financial loss if the team or star player doesn't win or, in the case of the *Oracle*, doesn't compete at all. If an athlete or team is involved in a scandal, such as drug use or questionable off-the-field activities, a sponsor is wise to examine whether it

Tony Volpentest was able to get the leg sockets he needed to sprint in the 1996 and 2000 Paralympics thanks to a sponsorship by billionaire businessman Ross Perot.

wants its company associated with that person or team. A sponsorship should include program advertisements, television and radio ads, signs in the venue, sales of products at the facility (such as samples), special seating for VIPs, autograph sessions, visits from top athletes, chances to watch the teams practice, and so on. Before companies or individuals decide to sponsor a sports team or club, they should carefully consider several marketing objectives, says the Bedford Consulting Group: "Building awareness and affinity with a key audience (team ownership or loyal fans); Modifying key corporate attributes (appeal to younger affluent adults, older conservative adults); Building business with team players (professional athletes); Selling product (ability to distribute brochures and applications in sports programs)."

When a single athlete is sponsored, this can help pay for training and living expenses in a job that doesn't pay a salary. A private sponsor is usually a wealthy individual who enjoys the sport and is willing to pay for some or all of an athlete's expenses. For example, billionaire Ross Perot's sponsorship of leg-amputee sprinter Tony Volpentest helped the athlete buy the leg sockets he needed to train for the Atlanta Paralympics in 1996. Corporate sponsors are more common. The athlete receives funding from the company while the company gets some publicity. (In an endorsement, the company does not pay for training costs.) Sometimes a company will own a whole team, too, which is another type of sponsorship.

HIGH SCHOOL AND COLLEGE GAME PLAN

An internship during high school or college is a fantastic way to learn about sports sponsoring and buying. An internship in some kind of advertising job can be a big help and may be a necessary step in applying for, and scoring, an entry-level position. Consider internships with businesses, especially in sales, to learn about commodities, prices, suppliers, and markets. Helpful and enlightening courses include marketing, psychology, accounting, and statistics.

THE CREATIVE ANGLE

Every person, place, or product in sports—Fenway Park, Shaun White, skateboards, or the USA Bobsled & Skeleton Federation—needs promotion. Plenty of jobs in sports marketing involve a lot of originality and imagination. Marketers should always be thinking about innovative ways to bring people's attention to their game, event, product, or athlete. Art, computer graphics, Web design, and writing are just a few of the creative angles to sports marketing.

Creative opportunities in sports marketing are plentiful: ads and brochures, newsletters, radio and television advertisements, and even coupons all need lively language and a vivid look. Web sites not only need energetic, engaging images and text, but they need to be updated regularly so the site will not seem stale and outdated to anyone who visits often.

In general, most (but by no means all) sports buyer and sponsor careers require a bachelor's or master's degree in engineering, business, economics, or one of the applied sciences. A master's degree is a good idea if the student wants to score a top-level purchasing manager position.

One can achieve entry-level positions as assistant media planner or assistant media buyer, but employers prefer applicants with a bachelor's degree, preferably with a major in marketing or advertising. Research jobs are nearly always scored by applicants with experience and a master's degree or higher, usually in marketing or statistics. Support services and administrative jobs depend on the type of job a particular company needs, so the work and its requirements differ between companies.

Plenty of entry-level positions do not necessarily require a degree, such as those in the creative department. Experience is helpful in getting these jobs. Assistant copywriter positions do not usually require a degree, but the Bureau of Labor Statistics (BLS) suggests that it can help with the demanding communication skills required in this position.

Buyers and sponsors should be good with people and able to communicate well. People in these fields are creative and are good problem solvers, too. Positions abroad or representing a foreign firm are common, so familiarity with foreign languages will be a big help. Another plus is that knowing foreign languages will help if working with minorities who are not fluent in English.

CAREERS IN BUYING AND SPONSORING

Careers in this category are located all over the country. Work hours generally follow a basic workday schedule, but extra hours in the evenings or on weekends may be necessary to meet a sales deadline. Compared to other industries, most of the jobs are full-time, with fewer part-time options. Some positions require some travel, too.

BUYERS

Buyers are in charge of deciding what their company will sell, according to the BLS. Buyers watch inventory and sales levels, keep an eye on the sales of competitors, and observe economic conditions to figure out what and how much consumers might buy in the future. Buyers should know how to forecast what consumers will want to buy. If their predictions aren't accurate, the company is stuck with a lot of inventory they can't sell. If they can't

Buyers for Tennessee's NBA Memphis Grizzlies team keep a sharp eye on items that fly off the shelves so they have them in stock and anticipate what may be popular.

sell it, they can't make back the money they invested, so there isn't much or any profit.

Wholesale and retail buyers buy items for resale. In sports, this might include clothing and items such as travel mugs or team jerseys showing a team logo or a star athlete's photograph. Purchasing agents buy merchandise and services that their company or group will use. For example, they may need to figure out how much customers will want to buy team logo baseball hats from their company as well as from any competing company that also

sells the hats. A buyer also has to think of other customers who might be interested in buying hats. He or she has to figure out how to sell the hats at a price that people will pay and that will also help the company make money.

MEDIA BUYERS

Media buyers are responsible for reaching deals for media-related sponsorships. They discuss deals and contracts and maintain good working relationships with contacts such as media representatives (or "reps"). Media buyers, according to JobsInSports.com, plan and make deals for paid television and radio ads, as well as print and other types of advertising. They also look for programs by other spon-

RIGHTS HOLDERS

Groups such as the International Olympic Committee, the National Football League, the National Collegiate Athletic Association, Major League Baseball, the National Basketball Association, and the United States Olympic Committee are just a few of the rights holders listed by John P. Bevilaqua. They own and manage events and competitions. Rights holders make money when television broadcasters make financial offers for the right to show these games. Broadcasters bid against each other for the privilege of gaining the right to show the programs, which makes money, known as rights fees, for the rights holders. The fees paid for the rights to broadcast an event keep increasing, but sponsors keep paying to have their names associated with these high-profile events and athletes. Over the past few years, this continued growth has slowed somewhat.

sors or vendors that might make money for events. Most buyers who are employed by large or medium-sized companies focus on purchasing at least two kinds of products. Buyers for smaller companies might be in charge of acquiring the company's entire inventory. Media buyers focus on where and when they can purchase air time for their advertisements. They bargain for a good deal to purchase the time and then confirm that the ads appear as scheduled. They are also responsible for forecasting rates, use, and budgets.

PURCHASING MANAGERS

At one time, event marketing was often done by the assistant athletic director or assistant sports information director. With so much money—not to mention their reputations—on the line, colleges and other companies choose their marketing managers a lot more carefully. These days, companies are making this an executive position. What a company buys or who it sponsors is crucial to maintaining its good name and its success.

A purchasing manager may be responsible for supervising other purchasing employees (known as purchasing agents) and may take on some of the more complicated purchases. Manufacturing companies sometimes call this position the purchasing director. Purchasing managers or directors sometimes use the Internet to put the word out about what they are looking to buy. They may also take bids and offers over the Internet.

Chapter 4
SPORTS PROMOTERS

If sports promoter seems like a good career choice, be very good at promoting. For a boxing promoter, for example, this means "knowing how to market and advertise a fight so that it appeals to the broadest possible demographic. It's knowing how to get the most paying customers to want to see the fight." The promoter wants to get sports fans and all kinds of other people to watch or attend the match. To make a profit, the promoter must promote, market, and publicize the event.

PRIME PROMOTERS

Don King is one sports promoter who is known by many people, and not just because of his wild hair. He has managed to package professional boxing events at large facilities, while craftily bargaining for television rights and getting the boxer an admirable prize. Don King, through his company, Don King Productions, has been

Flamboyant boxing promoter Don King (*right*) is known for his wild hair and colorful promotions of boxing events and athletes, such as featherweight world champion Elio Rojas.

an outrageously successful boxing promoter of more than five hundred world champion fights, and he has promoted famous boxers like "Big George" Foreman, "Iron Mike" Tyson, and "Sugar" Ray Leonard. And there are plenty more on his list of champions. He even promoted the great "Thrilla in Manila" match between Muhammad Ali and Joe Frazier in 1975. People around the world watched this match. In 2008 he was hired by Nike to promote "Grapple in the Apple," a U.S. Open tennis match between rivals Rafael Nadal and Roger Federer.

But of course, Don King isn't the only sports promoter out there. President of the Ultimate Fighting Championship (UFC) Dana White is a sports promoter who is involved with everything from event planning and marketing to public relations and broadcast production. In a way, Kathrine Switzer got her start as a sports promoter when she ran the Boston Marathon in 1967. A judge tried to physically shove her out of an all-male race, but she ran anyway. Switzer has been promoting women in sports ever since.

A sports manager can be confused with a sports promoter, but the two professions are very different. Managers look out for the good of the athlete, but the promoter might focus on making money for him- or herself. So when the headlines shout that a sports figure has won another title but soon after cry out about the same star's financial woes, it may be thanks to a crooked promoter. As in almost any career, there are some who do not play fairly. Sometimes these shady sports promoters make the headlines and overshadow so many who are fair and honest.

HIGH SCHOOL AND COLLEGE GAME PLAN

Consider an internship with a promoter during college or even high school. Because many sports promoters and related sports marketing positions are often filled with experienced employees from within the company, don't hesitate to take an entry-level position in a good company. It's a great way to learn the ropes and make connections.

Although lots of sports promoters work for themselves, others work for an employer. For management positions in promotions, employers are likely to recruit employees with a bachelor's degree or higher in business administration. Courses such as business law, economics, accounting, and mathematics might encourage an employer to take a second look at a résumé.

As with many jobs these days, there are some optional skills that give one an edge on the job hunt and might come in handy on the job, too. Computer skills can be a huge plus for the would-be sports promoter. Record keeping and maintaining data are both done on computers. Knowing how to use social media and the Internet is a bonus as well. Learning a foreign language is another good step. Some sports promoters travel all around the world or meet with clients. Spanish is an especially common language that might be useful.

With so much wheeling and dealing—with athletes, coaches, their managers, and the many people involved in

Sports promoters have to be comfortable with public speaking to promote their athletes or events. Activities such as debate clubs can help sharpen this skill and benefit anyone thinking of this career.

arranging an event—a sports promoter has to be able to talk the talk. So anyone interested in this field should be a good speaker and writer. Communication and writing skills will be a big asset. It may take time and practice, but a good sports promoter has to know not just what to say, but when, or when not, to say anything. Such skills can help make new connections and also maintain good relationships with current clients and staff.

Lots of promoters who work with firms go on to be managers. Naturally, there are not as many chances for advancement within the company in smaller firms, so getting promoted may take a bit longer than it might in a larger business.

CAREERS IN SPORTS PROMOTION

Sports promotion is sometimes called a "glamour" job, says Stateuniversity.com, because the promoters get to meet the teams and players. So competition for these jobs or, for entrepreneurs, getting top clients, is competitive and intense. But don't give up. Sports is one industry that has continued to grow over the years, and more job options will open up as long as this growth keeps up the pace.

SPORTS PROMOTIONS MANAGER

Promotions managers guide marketing programs that advertise and offer incentives to the buyer in hopes of boosting sales. A lot of these promotions use good, old-fashioned U.S. mail, ads in newspapers or on the Internet, displays right in the store or sports venue, product support, or other special events. Promotions can include discounts and coupons, samples, and contests.

Most sports promoters spend lots of time on the road, traveling to meet with athletes and coaches, potential and existing sponsors, and the media. This means evenings and weekends away from home, but a sports promotions manager does get to attend the games.

SPORTS AGENT

Many companies and teams hover around the athletes and coaches, in hope that the athletes or coaches will join their team or recommend their brand or product. A sports agent, also called athlete representative, represents the athlete when it comes time to bargain for a good contract, salary, endorsements, and other business arrangements. Enter the sports agent. A sports agent looks out for the athlete or coach.

There are many ways to get into the sports agent field, says sports agent Darren Heitner. "Political Science classes taught me how to think outside of the box and argue my point when there was no true right or wrong answer. Mass Communication allowed me to understand the value and best techniques of advertising, public relations, cyberspace marketing, etc. Geography made me

Tom Cruise played one of the most memorable sports agent roles in the film *Jerry Maguire*, as someone who follows his own values and does right by his players in a highly competitive industry.

worldlier. Each has helped out in its own unique way." Variety is the spice of life, the old saying goes, and a variety of courses will help prepare you for a career as a sports agent, as well as other careers in sports marketing.

"Show me the money!" shouts Tom Cruise as the main character in the movie *Jerry Maguire*. He plays a hard-hitting sports agent who has no choice but to go out on his own when he decides to stick with his values. One of the toughest yet most rewarding parts of the job for Darren Heitner is knowing he is helping his client by being ethical. It might make for some sleepless nights, worrying that rival agents are using risky, even dangerous, means to promote their clients. But in the end, when an athlete affirms that Heitner's work has helped him or her out, he knows he has been fair and honest. He told a reporter at Sportsmanagementdegree.org, "Make sure to work hard, put in countless hours of work, and think outside of the box to add value for the people that surround you."

SPORTS PROMOTIONS DIRECTOR

Lots of promoters who work with firms go on to be managers and directors. Naturally, there are not as many chances for advancement within the company in smaller firms, so getting promoted may take a bit longer than it might in a larger business.

Sports teams and school athletic departments often hire sports promotions directors (and development directors) to plan and employ promotions that will encourage and boost ticket sales. They also work with advertisers and athletic equipment companies in hopes of encouraging them to sponsor the team or sports department by paying to advertise their products or company at events.

SPORTS PROMOTER, ENTREPRENEUR

Sports promoters are busy people. A lot of the time, sports promoters create their own events. They basically arrange and pay for everything, including making sure everything is legally sound. Sometimes sports promoters find other investors to help pay for an event to make sure the event can afford everything from napkins to referees to ticket sales to advertising. Promoters of star athletes usually hire lots of other people to take care of the details, but lesser known star promoters do it all (or mostly) themselves. No matter how famous the athlete, though, the promoter takes responsibility if anything goes wrong.

Because they are financially accountable for so much, promoters have a lot on the line. They make their money from the event's profits, of course, and will likely make money just for their athlete performing, whether or not he or she wins. Even more money is up for grabs if their athlete is the winner and takes the prize.

Chapter 5

SPORTS PUBLIC RELATIONS

In a nutshell, public relations (PR) careers are directed toward making sure a company, business, or individual is seen in a good light in the public eye. Sometimes this involves writing press releases. Press releases make sure the media knows about upcoming games, when a sports star does some volunteer work, or when a stadium donates the profits from a certain game to a charity.

CREATING THE SHARPER IMAGE

Public relations can also involve smoothing over rough spots when a company does or says something controversial. A press release manager or specialist might have to explain the rationale behind its company's or executive's actions or business plans. Or maybe, when for some reason things have gone very wrong, the public relations department does damage control in hopes of preventing any more harm to the company's or athlete's reputation

Students who are interested in public relations for sports marketing should be comfortable promoting their team or product to all kinds of new people.

than absolutely necessary. Sometimes, this is called putting a positive spin on things. Most of the time, though, people in the PR department are concerned with getting the events and actions of a company or star into the news and thus out to the public so that they want to buy the company product, come to the team game, or buy tickets to the athlete's appearances and tournaments.

Technically, sports public relations careers are not in the sports marketing department. However, the work overlaps quite a bit with marketing in its common goal: to put forth the best image of a company or individual, which in turn (hopefully) encourages the public to buy the products and attend the games. If a team, venue, or athlete is not viewed favorably or—much worse some would say—not in the news at all, sports fan are less likely to support them. Public relations departments work together with advertising and marketing, as well as sales, to make sure marketing research and strategies, sales and advertising, promotion, pricing, and product development are all coordinated. Public relations specialists also make sure everyone—consumers, shareholders, and employees, as well as managers—is informed and on the same page about the products and policies of a company.

People in public relations are often quite creative and some change careers to become journalists because that field provides a more creative outlet. However, many journalists become public relations employees because the salary is much better. In addition to creativity and communication skills, an outstanding PR candidate should like talking and communicating with other people. An outgoing personality is a huge plus because so much of PR involves talking to other people, whether the media, sports teams, or star athletes and coaches.

HIGH SCHOOL AND COLLEGE GAME PLAN

As with any career in sports, consider an internship. For those interested in the PR field, go for an internship involving any sort of public relations. This way, students get a hands-on education about the ins and outs of PR work and gain experience that will improve their chances of getting that all-important entry-level job. Another option is to become a member of the Public Relations Student Society of America, which is associated with the Public Relations Society of America. In student chapters of the International Association of Business Communicators, students can chat with and learn from public relations specialists and network with professionals. Professional contacts could help them find a full-time job after they've completed their degree.

Some colleges do offer a specific degree in public relations, according to Princetonreview.com, but few employers look only for a degree when searching for the perfect PR person for their sports team. Instead, go for what Stephanie Hofmann calls "more breadth than depth." What she means is that a broad education may prove far more useful than a very specific course of study in the long run. Jobs in PR require an employee to be familiar with more than just the sport or athlete in question. (Also, a wider variety of classes will help if in a few years a new profession or life focus seems like a good move and may prevent a whole new degree being necessary.)

For those searching for PR jobs, BLS indicates that a degree in journalism, public relations, or another field in communications will likely provide the best chance of getting into the public relations game. If an internship seems like an appealing option during high school or college, look for those in public relations. It can be with a sports PR person or someone who does PR for another type of business. The experience in PR is key. Similar related work experience is also a big plus. Without a suitable education or job experience, public relations jobs may be hard to score.

Those with an eye on the public relations manager career should aim for degrees in communications, journalism, or English. Try to include courses in advertising, business administration, public affairs, and political science. Great writing and speaking skills will help in any public relations career.

CAREERS IN SPORTS PUBLIC RELATIONS

The main careers in public relations are PR specialist and PR manager. But don't be put off by a lack of options. It's true that there are more job seekers applying for public relations jobs than there are actual positions. However, the Bureau of Labor Statistics predicts job growth in this field over the next decade. Remember that there are some steps that can help would-be publicists on their way to a career in guiding and boosting the reputations of the U.S. Olympic Curling Team, a tennis star such as Venus or Serena Williams, or a minor league baseball team such as Washington State's Tacoma Rainiers.

Even a top-ranked tennis pro like Serena Williams needs a public relations manager to make sure she maintains a good image and a positive relationship with the public.

PUBLIC RELATIONS SPECIALIST

Public relations specialists—also known as communications specialists and media specialists, among other names—advocate, or go to bat, for organizations such as companies, colleges, and even hospitals. And PR specialists

HITTING A HOME RUN

Experience, ability, and leadership are keys to getting a promotion in sports marketing jobs, but they are by no means the only options for hitting home runs on the job. Some large companies offer management training programs. Lots of good-sized businesses also offer options for continuing education. Some may be offered at the company office (known as in-house) or at local colleges and universities. Seminars and conferences presented by professional organizations are also often promoted and suggested by corporations. Colleges and universities frequently work with lots of marketing associations and the like to fund management training programs on both the national and local levels. They tend to include courses such as international marketing, sales management, telemarketing, product promotion, marketing communication, and market research. Lots of companies will foot the bill for employees who take (and complete) these courses and training programs.

give managers advice about strategies and policies. In the sports world, this also translates into ensuring a good public image for teams, venues, and athletes, too. Every sports team or athlete wants a good relationship with the public. The public relations specialist is there to help make sure that happens, even when things aren't looking so good.

Princetonreview.com describes public relations as "a good career for the generalist. A PR person must keep up with current events and be well versed in pop culture to understand what stories will get the public's attention. It takes a combination of analysis and creative problem solving to get a client in the public eye." This type of work is always new, and the challenges are always changing and often unexpected. Careers in PR mean dealing a lot with the media, lots of writing (such as press releases), research, keeping contracts up-to-date, and responding to inquiries. Anyone who does PR for an athlete or coach—or even a small team or venue—has to deal with pretty much everything from contacting people, planning and executing research, and advertising and promoting (which may be in cooperation with a specific marketing department). The main executive in PR is often the vice president, who develops overall plans and policies with other executives.

Although the BLS reports that there are a fair number of entry-level jobs in public relations, there are likely to be more qualified people than there are available positions. Such high-profile jobs are often in great demand and thus can be a challenge to land. Social media is becoming more prevalent in marketing, and it may actually increase the number of PR jobs. Sports PR specialists use Twitter, Facebook, and Google+ to get the word out about their teams, players, games, and events. Knowing how to use these medias effectively can make a job seeker more desirable.

On the job, a PR specialist can expect a bustling office with lots of activity. Although most PR offices are in large

Public relations departments use social media such as Twitter and Facebook to connect and interact with team fans and keep them informed about game schedules and special events.

cities such as New York and Chicago, it is becoming more common for offices to be spread across the nation, closer to their clients. Most employees work a basic eight-hour day, but expect plenty of unpaid overtime, too. Some sports PR specialists need to be on-call in case of an emergency or disaster. They attend games, meetings, and community events. Sometimes traveling is part of the job as well.

PUBLIC RELATIONS MANAGER

Public relations managers are in charge of planning and guiding public relations programs to produce and maintain a positive public image for an employer or client. So a PR manager for a sports venue might write press releases to alert the media about upcoming games. A PR manager for a corporation that manufactures running shoes might arrange to sponsor a corporate event, such as a local race. This kind of sponsorship helps preserve and enhance the company's public appearance and character. PR managers are responsible for making sure the public, and their main

New York Yankees third baseman Alex Rodriguez (*sitting far right*) speaks to reporters at a news conference. A public relations manager might arrange a news conference so a team or athlete can make an important announcement.

audience, knows their point of view. They keep a sharp eye on all kinds of trends that might concern their company and make suggestions on how to best market the company based on what they think the trends will be. Lots of PR managers focus on a specific type of business, such as sports or music, or on a specific area, such as managing crises.

Most PR managers work in an office setting, near the top executives. There can be a lot of pressure to meet deadlines. Long hours and working more than a forty-hour work week can be pretty common, too. In the case of sports, public relations managers might have to attend games that run late. They may be at the mercy of a team's schedule, which might take them across the country and back in a couple of days. Many PR managers travel for meetings with customers and to consult with other public relations personnel.

Chapter 6

SPORTS BROADCASTING

Sports broadcasting tends to make people think about voices and personalities, such as the humorous Greg Gumbel, or maybe Red Barber's quirky baseball game expressions such as "can of corn" and "Oh Doctor!" come to mind. But sports broadcasting is more than a nifty turn of phrase. It's even more than being able to use all-around sports knowledge. Each of these talents is all well and good, but they go nowhere without the video and audio recordings, computer know-how, or engineering behind the scenes that puts them on the air to broadcast the games, athletes, and sports news to eager viewers and listeners. Writers pen the witty advertisements and news stories that hopefully entice the audience to tune in to the next game or buy the team's latest athletic gear. And whether the broadcaster is marketing the latest big game, the hottest athlete, or the newest energy bar, Harry Caray's quote rings true: "It's the fans that need spring

One of the most sought-after careers in sports broadcasting is the television broadcaster. Sports analysts Greg Gumbel, Greg Anthony, and Seth Davis discuss the game's plays and players, which keeps viewers tuned in.

training. You gotta get 'em interested. Wake 'em up and let 'em know that their season is coming, the good times are gonna roll." All of sports broadcasting is geared toward getting people excited about nearly every aspect of sports.

BROADCASTING BASICS

When someone says they have a career in sports broadcasting, most people immediately think of the booming voices that announce the plays over the airwaves and the lively personalities who give listeners and viewers the lowdown on the top players and team game strategies. These broadcasters announce the exciting play-by-plays, interview coaches and athletes, and discuss the details of the games after the final scores have been settled. The broadcasters often research, write, and deliver their own coverage of television and radio sports events and shows.

In reality, however, most sports broadcasting jobs are behind the scenes. Besides the anchor and announcer positions, sports broadcasting jobs include producers, video editors, salespeople, news directors, and station managers, to name just a few. Every one of these jobs contribute to getting the sports news, events, and stories on the air.

Sports broadcasters advertise sporting events and games to audiences through television and radio. And advertisers pay fees for commercial time when the broadcast is aired. Broadcasting also involves television and radio stations as well as networks that either generate content or purchase the rights to broadcast programs that have already been recorded. Advertising sales agents, also called account executives, sell advertising time to sponsors, advertising agencies, and other buyers. Producers and announcers, who make up some of the production staff, help produce sports news and programs as well.

Sports news and programs, on both television and radio, are popular and attract a large audience. Everyone wants to check in and hear the latest on their favorite teams. And as a result, these broadcasts usually make a lot of money, so the fees that the networks pay are more than earned back. Johnny K. Lee, writer for the *Sports Journal*, reports, "For instance, NBC, a national American broadcasting company, paid the sum of $3.5 billion to receive the right to transmit five Olympic games for the period of 2000–2008." And before the games even started, NBC had made back its money, and then some, by selling advertising.

Sports advertising sales agents, or account executives, are in charge of selling advertising time to sponsors, advertising agencies, and other buyers. To best sell their advertising time, sales representatives need to know details about their network's or station's audience, including how much money they make, whether men or women watch, their ages, and what sorts of things they buy. Stations can earn money by broadcasting from a local business, such as a gym. Stations can hold special promotions at games, too, where they can set up a booth and pass out stickers, pins, or other advertising merchandise. They can also post big posters or signs to bring attention to their station or specific sports shows.

Because sports broadcasting depends on the games, the work schedule can be a little crazy. It might mean working from the crack of dawn (or even before) or into the wee hours of the night, depending on the game times and locations. A fair amount of travel might be involved as well. Jobs in sales might be stressful, too, because there is a lot of pressure to reach sales goals. However, such jobs are more likely to be in a basic office setting.

HIGH SCHOOL AND COLLEGE GAME PLAN

Sports broadcasting is extremely competitive—especially for on-air positions—so to get a foot in the door, experience is important. So many people are trying to get these jobs that a lot of employers will not offer on-the job training. But do not despair. Many high schools offer lots of opportunities. Many have audio-visual or media clubs that offer excellent chances to get some broadcasting experience. Others even have their own closed-circuit television or radio stations. Some high schools have announcers for their games, too. If the school has a newspaper, look into writing articles, especially those that feature sports events or athletes. Classes in public speaking, drama, and foreign languages might be helpful options as well. During the summer, there are sports broadcasting camps where campers can try out play-by-play announcing, make an anchor tape, and learn from broadcasting celebrities.

Outside of school, internships and jobs might be available at local or even professional television and radio stations. Even though many of these positions do not come with a paycheck, they might offer college credit or even tuition. The experience gained from these jobs and internships is the most valuable part, though. The chance to get

Even unpaid internships can result in experience and some great connections. A résumé listing some actual broadcasting experience in front of or behind the camera is likely to get noticed.

hands-on experience in almost any aspect of broadcasting, especially under the supervision of skilled radio and television professionals, will go a long way when applying for jobs. Meeting new people in the industry, even if not directly in the sports marketing department, always helps, too. College degrees in communications and journalism will go a long way toward helping get a first job in broadcasting.

Because networking is so important, joining professional sports, broadcasting, or marketing organizations is a great way to meet other people in the industry. These

RADIO TO THE RESCUE

When a sporting event does not seem to be selling tickets very well, a well-placed advertisement on the radio or television can make all the difference. In his book *How Did I Get Here?*, Tony Hawk describes his first skateboarding show, the Boom Boom HuckJam, which wasn't selling many tickets. At first they were going to "paper the house," or give away lots of tickets to fill the seats. The benefit of this strategy is that the event wouldn't look like it bombed when the press reported on it. Instead, the show's promoter went straight to the local radio stations. Those station promotions made all the difference. As more people heard the station talk up the show on the air, more of them bought tickets and filled many of the seats. Bigger television networks such as MTV and ESPN covered the Boom Boom HuckJam and gave it great reviews. This gave future shows even more publicity.

Skateboarder Tony Hawk's marketing team went straight to radio stations to get the word out about the Boom Boom HuckJam. Tickets sold, and the HuckJam got some great publicity.

groups also offer opportunities to learn about changes and new technologies in the field. Some organizations publish newsletters in print and online.

CAREERS IN SPORTS BROADCASTING

Like many careers in sports marketing, most broadcasting jobs require a background and training in the basics. To get a position as a sports video editor, for example, the idea of putting together video with music and special effects should be interesting, whether the videos are about sports or fashion. Love of sports is great, but the core of the job is what should be most interesting.

BEHIND THE SCENES TECHNICIANS

Sports commentators and reporters could not get the word out about sports games and news without their camera operators, recording engineers, and computer administrators—just to name a few of the behind-the-scenes technicians. Electronic equipment is a necessity in today's broadcasts. Technical positions may require only a high school diploma or some brief training. That said, some stations want an employee who has had some experience with broadcast technology, electronics, or engineering from a four-year college. As computers and digital technology

Some great broadcasting careers happen behind the camera. The more experience a student can get with modern electronic technologies, the better his or her chances become of landing a job.

become more prevalent, however, the more experience an employee has in those areas, the better.

BROADCASTING MANAGER

Managerial positions usually require training, and many stations prefer four-year bachelor's degrees and training in broadcast technology, electronics, or engineering. Some courses to consider might include audio production, mass media, broadcast journalism, media writing, and communication law. Some schools require students to complete a concentration, dual degree, or minor in another area that is associated with sports. Other programs require students to study human movement, or kinesiology, as well.

BROADCASTING

Helpful degrees for broadcasting include broadcasting, journalism, and communications. Some trade schools teach announcing for television and radio, as well as production and sports writing. Unfortunately, some broadcasting colleges do not have the best reputations. Before enrolling, be sure to thoroughly research the school's background and academic status through organizations such as the Bureau of Labor Statistics.

When first getting into the broadcasting job market, many entry-level positions are often available at smaller television and radio stations. Competition for these positions tends to be fierce in larger cities, though. Smaller stations may have limited opportunities, so be prepared to change employers—and locations, possibly to other parts of the country—to advance into positions of higher responsibility and salary. Sometimes taking a non-broadcasting job within the station is a good way to get established and gain the experience needed to move into broadcasting positions. Some sports broadcasters even go on to host their own shows on television or the radio.

Broadcasting is an excellent way to get consumer attention for everything from running shoes to thirst-quenching energy drinks to the games and matches themselves. One of the beauties of the broadcasting niche of marketing is that there are job opportunities for lots of different people with various strengths and interests. There are jobs for sports enthusiasts who want to be back in the office writing the news stories or designing advertisements and promotions, behind the camera shooting the pulse-racing moments as the ball swishes through the hoop to win the game, or on the sidelines giving a play-by-play of the quarterback who rushes toward the end zone.

Chapter 7

SPORTS FACILITY AND VENUE MARKETING

A ll the marketing of sports, athletes, and products is a waste of time if the players don't have a place to compete and the spectators can't come together to cheer on their favorite teams and athletes. Facilities and venues are places where players compete and people can come watch them. With cable television, pay-per-view shows, and Internet live streaming, it's often easier on the wallet and more convenient with a busy schedule to stay home on the couch and watch the action from there.

FILL THE STANDS

Performing arts are often grouped together with spectator sports. Sports organizations create or manage and advertise live presentations involving the performances of athletes. Like performing arts centers, sports venues present the events. They arrange, supervise, and market the games and feature events. They also oversee and represent entertainers. Finally, the venue supplies the artistic and technical talents needed to take the events to the field or the stage.

Although a little marketing can go a long way, Melvin Helitzer, author of *The Dream Job: Sports Publicity, Promotion and Marketing*, estimates that more than $4 billion is spent on sports events sponsorships.

Sports venues are categorized as "arts, entertainment, and recreation" and are grouped in as part of the "live performances or events segment" on the Bureau of Labor Statistics Web site, bls.gov. This includes professional sports, of course, and also establishments such as athletic clubs, which offer sports facilities and equipment to amateurs. Commercial sports clubs are usually available to amateur and professional athletes. Such clubs promote and market events for just about any sport imaginable: soccer, boxing, volleyball, gymnastics, water polo, and orienteering are just a few. There are even auto racing clubs. Companies that promote both amateur and pro sports are often included in this part of the industry, too.

HIGH SCHOOL AND COLLEGE GAME PLAN

Plenty of options exist for the student who wants to get a foot in the door of venue sports marketing, even as early as high school. As with any area of sports marketing, the key is to gain familiarity with marketing in general. So

Sports stadiums offer a lot of opportunities for a student interested in marketing. Ticket and merchandise sales are two basic options, but internships are often available in the marketing department, too.

if a job or internship at a sports stadium isn't an option during high school or college, getting some experience in a ticketing or marketing department for another sort of performance venue will still provide a great deal of hands-on education.

During high school and college, consider selling merchandise at venues. To get an upper-level marketing or director job, try offering to do an unpaid internship at an local venue, whether its focus is on sports, theater, or some other type of recreation and entertainment. Sometimes seasonal jobs and internships are short-term options to try out a different type of venue without so much commitment. The high school and college years might be good times to check out different types of stadiums and fields. Each one will provide one more type of experience to add to a résumé, too.

College is naturally the time to start focusing more on classes that will enhance a career in sports marketing for venues and facilities. Nearly every manager of a sports venue has a four-year college degree in business administration or liberal arts under his or her belt. Most have gone on to complete a master's or a doctoral degree as well. A focus on and familiarity with marketing and business is a tremendous asset because promoting events makes up a significant part of the work.

Marketing a sports facility or venue is often considered part of the hospitality business. In fact, some colleges put sports marketing in the hospitality school. This may seem like an odd categorization at first, but is it really? Stadiums are in the business of making their facilities welcoming. Their events aim to be fun and entertaining—a welcome break from work and school for everyone. Definitely research potential colleges and be sure they are accredited and seem like a comfortable place to study. Online courses are a good option for anyone who wants to study from home or needs to schedule around another job. The sports marketing programs that are offered in the hospitality division of the college should not be over-looked.

For public speaking abilities that shine, the Toastmasters organization is a good place to look. At Toastmasters meetings, one can improve his or her speaking and leadership skills without feeling intimidated.

CAREERS IN VENUE AND FACILITY MARKETING

To get people into the stands of sports complexes, stadiums, and fields, the venues have to advertise. The sports venues that stage the games need to make a profit to stay afloat, of course, says John P. Bevilaqua. "This model is particularly evident in professional sports where the local team sells in-stadium advertising and tickets and, on occasion, local broadcast rights, thus providing additional revenue to the host team or facility or owner." More people in the stands obviously means more ticket sales, and it also means more purchases of crispy french fries and icy sodas and souvenirs such as T-shirts and hats during a game.

TICKET SALES

Some enthusiastically advocate for getting into ticket sales as a first job after college or even during high school as a

One of the main goals of a stadium's marketing department is to get fans into the seats to watch the game. Venue managers also arrange events and coordinate fund-raising.

summer or weekend job. It can be the first step up into a career in sports, but it is by no means the only way to get into venue marketing. There are plenty of steps that will lead a job seeker straight to higher-level marketing jobs, but those are not options that work for everyone. Ticketing operations jobs are available at just about every stadium and field, as well as sports museums and for sports conferences of all kinds.

VENUE MANAGER

Much of the marketing of sports venues is done by managers. The manager also has other duties, of course, which may include arranging events and fund-raising, just to name a couple. Special events such as tournaments always need a director to organize and market them. Administration positions for the enthusiastic sports marketer include sports club manager and promoter. Fitness centers and sports facilities always need marketing to get the word out about the sports programs. Sales positions are often open for sporting goods manufacturers, too. Many

THE GLITZ AND THE GRUNT WORK

Part of the excitement of marketing an event or facility is meeting the athletes. What a thrill it is to meet sports stars, whether local or international, and walk out onto the field while the players warm up. Meeting celebrities is a bigger part of some careers than others, but stars always go to the stadiums. Stephanie Hofmann recounts an opportunity when she was the one-to-one for volleyball star Holly McPeak. McPeak was the top volleyball player at the time, so Hofmann was pretty excited to spend the day with her. Hofmann's responsibilities for the day included jobs such as picking up McPeak at the airport and driving her to interviews. After all we said and done, what does Hofmann remember most? "All of the grunt work. A lot of grunt work!"

At other high-profile events, Hofmann remembers that after the lights go down, and the stars and cheering audience go home, there is still a lot of work to do. At Volley Across America, the event for the one hundredth anniversary of volleyball, her company staged an event in New York City's Central Park. To make room for all the volleyball nets, they had to break down hundreds of folding chairs. After the heart-racing volleying was over, the staff worked long into the night to put the chairs all back in place. Sure, there is excitement and even glamour in marketing sports events and venues, but remember that glitz comes hand in hand with plenty of good, old-fashioned hard work.

stadiums have a clubhouse, and often it employs its own manager, who promotes that feature of the venue.

An executive in a smaller venue might have responsibilities that include advertising, promotions, sales, and public relations. Sometimes an executive vice president's responsibilities include the venue's marketing and public relations policies. Account executives at a facility manage the venue's account services department and figure out how much advertising it needs. People in these positions should have stellar people skills. They need the ability to think logically and make firm decisions. All executives should be good leaders.

Executives can expect to work in an office setting and to spend long hours or weekends there to meet deadlines and sales goals. Luckily, many executives often have large, open offices. Traveling around the country and even around the world to meet with clients is fairly common. Sometimes an executive has a flexible schedule to make up for long hours or time away from home. Executives are under tremendous pressure to do a good job. If the facility is not doing well, the executive is often held responsible.

Don't be discouraged by an entry-level job. There will be plenty of opportunities to move up. To cruise up the corporate ladder, consider additional training programs, which may be offered at the company or at outside educational institutes. These programs teach management skills that can help an employee succeed.

Chapter 8

SPORTS EVENT MANAGEMENT AND OPERATIONS MARKETING

O nce the sports facility is booked and promoted, the marketing is far from done. A big-time event like the Superbowl can raise millions of dollars. John P. Bevilaqua notes, "in the case of the Olympics, these local organizing committees are created for a short duration during which they create their own infrastructure, rent facilities, organize competitions, sell tickets, stage events and then effectively go out of business, all in the span of approximately six to seven years." The events themselves need a lot of marketing, and it takes a lot of work to make sure they go on without a hitch.

But sports events are actually more than the games and tournaments. An event can include a fund-raiser or activity to raise awareness for a cause or disease. The MS Walk is held by the National Multiple Sclerosis Society to raise money for research. Events can include special promotions. A promotion can be a tractor trailer parked at the X Games with stations where fans can play the latest PlayStation *Shaun White Skateboarding* game. This kind of promotion lets users try out the game and see how cool it is. Then hopefully they buy it. Another kind of promotion is when a model approaches people at a game and asks them to try a sample of a product, such as a new sports drink.

CREATING EXCITEMENT

Managing and operating sports facilities and venues alone is a business. Selling tickets, team gear and products, and snacks and drinks all come into play for an event to bring in additional money and get people revved up about the event. When companies spend money to have their name associated with a sporting event, the companies generate that fan excitement and directly access the crowds. They reap the benefits of having their name or logo on radio, television, or print advertisements and again printed on game programs, schedules, and other items before, during, and even after the event.

The imagination may be the only limit to the number of ways a company can market its product or athlete at a venue, but they do have to be creative. These days, companies aim to grab more than just the audience.

SMART SMARTPHONE MARKETING

With so many sports fans keeping track of games on their cell phones and other mobile devices, more marketers are moving from big and loud to smaller and more personal ads. Major League Baseball already has an "At Bat" app that lets users follow many aspects of the game. Stadiums have been using text-to-screen messaging, which is when fans use their cell phones to send messages that are shown either on their own or combined for a poll on television or a scoreboard.

But text-to-screen messaging is only the beginning of a new and constantly improving way for companies to market directly to their consumers. Companies such as Volkswagen, Subway, and Verizon are all trying out more advanced marketing methods that use cell phones. Advertising has been used in everything from virtual games and contests to polling team fans. When these methods are used during an event, the company and the team can follow up by sending participating fans a text message with offers of discounts and special deals.

They also try to tie in with retailers and others. These days, collectibles—toys, gadgets, clothing, you name it—are all the rage. For example, a fan can get a nodding "bobblehead" figure of almost any famous sports star from baseball's Evan Longoria of the Tampa Bay Rays to NASCAR's Danica Patrick.

"Bobblehead" dolls of popular athletes, such NBA rookie guard Tyreke Evans, have been a hugely popular marketing tool for teams, athletes, and their retail partners.

One example Phil Schaaf, author of *Sports Marketing: It's Not Just a Game Anymore*, offers is that of Nabisco, which has many brands of food and snacks, such as Planters Peanuts and LifeSavers candy, just to name a couple. Together with the major retailer Target, Nabisco sponsored the Oakland A's major league baseball team. Their marketing plan included a series of Collector Kaps splashed with bright pictures of the teams, players, and coaches (with reproductions of their autographs) on the front and the product logos on the back. The hats were flashy and fun, but they were much more than that. Nabisco and Target released four sets of six images throughout the baseball season, emphasizing their relationship and expanding their marketing throughout the year, rather than just up to and at the event. The hats could even be redeemed as coupons at Target stores or kept as mementos.

HIGH SCHOOL AND COLLEGE GAME PLAN

During high school and college, look around during some of the team games and see how advertising in the gym or stadium could work. If the school has a store, offer to brainstorm and execute ideas for marketing water bottles with the school logo, or whatever the store sells. School events—school games, dances, and con-

One way to gain experience in marketing is to help your school store promote their merchandise. Items such as T-shirts, mugs, and other products bearing the team logo can sell fast.

certs—could be marketed with ads on a simple poster near a high-traffic area or on a digital scoreboard. These may seem like simple steps, but they all add up to experience that will be helpful when it comes time to decide on a college or job. If marketing at school was enjoyable, this could be a satisfying career.

Internships at hotels, stadiums, or other local sports facilities should offer some insight into how they market and organize their events. As with any career in sports or marketing, use these internships or jobs as chances to get to know as many people as possible. They may be good connections one day or could offer a recommendation for a future job. Learn as much as possible about the details of the marketing jobs there, too.

If college seems like a good plan, some universities actually offer specific degrees in sports and event management (SEM). At Elon University, for example, a student can expect to learn "the fundamentals of facility planning and maintenance; important terminology, philosophies and the evolution of the sport and event management industry; relevant contemporary issues; principles of special event programming; and marketing. SEM majors also take classes that examine concepts such as finance, accounting, communication, research strategies, and legal issues such as contracts, personal and product liability, negligence and risk management." Learning about hospitality as well as basic marketing, economics, accounting, and business will be a huge plus, too, and will be beneficial for marketing job opportunities outside of sports. Most employers look favorably on computer skills, of course, with so much bookkeeping and data stored on computers and the increasingly Internet-based marketing strategies. Strong writing and related communication skills are a plus, and so are Internet or social media know-how.

CAREERS IN EVENT MANAGEMENT AND OPERATIONS MARKETING

Venues offer a wide variety of job options. Like facility marketing jobs, ticketing is one way to get a foot in the door at the entry level of a good venue. A product demonstrator is another good way to start gaining experience and meeting other people at the venue.

EVENT MANAGER

Event managers are in the thick of things when it comes to event marketing. They work with managers in the advertising and promotions departments to get the word out and generate excitement for the company's events. Managers in product development and market research may work with the event manager to get an idea of how many people would be interested in coming to the events, what kinds of events might be popular in the future, and the types of events their competitors are holding. Event marketing managers also plan pricing so that the event makes money and the sports teams, athletes, or other clients also make a satisfactory profit. Promotions managers for an event lead programs to boost sales by blending advertising with purchasing incentives. Most event managers work in an office setting, usually near where the events

At a big stadium, such as the Staples Center, the special events coordinator might take care of smaller events while the venue manager arranges the major games for the most popular teams.

take place. The job can be stressful and heavily dependent on deadlines. Quite a bit of travel can be involved, too.

SPECIAL EVENTS COORDINATOR

Sometimes a venue has a manager to work on the large events at the facility, but that person can't do everything.

Enter the special events coordinator. A large venue such as the Staples Center might host one hundred or more smaller events every month, which include events of every size. The special events coordinator is an entry-level position. It can be good experience for a managerial job because the position offers a view of all the events from the ground up. Smaller facilities don't usually have a special events coordinator, so look toward larger sports stadiums for this kind of position. At smaller venues, the public relations personnel sometimes do this job. The special events coordinator is in charge of nearly every detail of an event from the planning to kickoff.

This is a position that can include a lot of travel and long hours, including weekends. Be prepared with good communication skills both to talk and write to a lot of people as the events are arranged. Have lots of energy to work on many events at the same time.

PRODUCT DEMONSTRATOR

Because event marketing can include promotions that offer samples or other chances to try out a product, entry-level jobs may include handing out samples at games or other events. The products may be exciting, but they need employees to draw in potential customers to try the energy bar or play the new game.

At some venues, there may be a team of demonstrators for larger events. Get ready for a lot of standing and walking. In this position the individual approaches customers at the venue and talks to them about the product. Good communication skills will help put a positive spin on the product or event being promoted. Long hours, weekends, and evenings are a large part of this job. This might be a good job during high school or college, too, and an opportunity to get in on the ground floor of a good company.

COLLEGE AND UNIVERSITY PROGRAMS IN SPORTS MARKETING

The following is a list of a number of colleges and universities that offer programs in sports marketing:

Baylor University, Waco, TX: sports sponsorship and sales

Bowling Green State University, Bowling Green, OH: sports management

California State University, Craig School of Business, Fresno, CA: sports marketing

Georgia Southern University, Statesboro, GA: sport management M.S.

Indiana University, Bloomington, IN: department of kinesiology, sports marketing and management program

Ithaca College, Ithaca, NY: sports management

New York University, New York, NY: school of continuing and professional studies, M.S. in sports business

Duquesne University, Palumbo Donahue School of Business, Pittsburgh, PA: sports marketing

Sacred Heart University, John F. Welch College of Business, Fairfield, CT: sports management

Syracuse University, David B. Falk College of Sport and Human Dynamics Department of Sports Management, Syracuse, NY: Sport management

United States Sports Academy, Daphne, AL:

bachelor of sports science, sports management

University of Arizona, Tucson, AZ: Eller College of Management, sports management

University of Houston, Houston, TX: C. T. Bauer College of Business marketing communications

University of Michigan, Ann Arbor, MI: sport business association

University of Minnesota, School of Kinesiology, Minneapolis, MN: sports management

University of Oregon, Lundquist College of Business, Warsaw Sports Marketing Center, Eugene, OR: sports marketing

The Wharton School, University of Pennsylvania, Philadelphia, PA: marketing and operations management

SPORTS MARKETING CAREERS AT A GLANCE

SPORTS BUYERS AND SPONSORS

BASIC DEGREES AND SKILLS

- Bachelor's or master's degree in engineering, business, economics, or an applied science

- Major in marketing or advertising

- Internet and social media skills

- Communication skills

- Foreign languages

BUYERS

- Decide what their company will sell

- Acquire inventory

- Keep track of inventory and sales levels

- Watch economic trends

SPORTS MEDIA BUYERS

- Reach deals for media-related sponsorships

- Discuss deals and contracts and maintain

good working relationships with media representatives (or "reps")

- Plan and negotiate paid ads for television, radio, print, and outdoor displays

PURCHASING MANAGERS

- Take on complicated purchases
- Take bids and offers over the Internet
- Supervise other purchasing employees

SPORTS PROMOTERS

BASIC DEGREES AND SKILLS

- Bachelor's or master's degree in business administration with a marketing emphasis
- Background in business law, management, economics, accounting, finance, mathematics, or statistics
- Computer skills
- Social media and Internet skills
- Foreign languages
- Communication and writing skills

SPORTS PROMOTIONS MANAGER

- Guide marketing programs

- Advertise and offer incentives

- Meet with athletes and coaches, sponsors, and media

SPORTS PROMOTIONS DIRECTOR

- Plan and employ promotions

- Work with advertisers and athletic equipment companies to gain sponsors

SPORTS PROMOTER, ENTREPRENEUR

- Market, promote, and advertise an event

- Arrange and pay for everything, including making sure everything is legally sound

SPORTS PUBLIC RELATIONS

BASIC DEGREES AND SKILLS

- Bachelor's in public relations, journalism, English, business, or communications

- Experience or background in advertising, business administration, public affairs, public speaking, political science

- Creative and technical writing

- Communications

- Social media and Internet skills

PUBLIC RELATIONS SPECIALIST

- Advocate for the team or athlete

- Maintain a good public image for teams, venues, and athletes

PUBLIC RELATIONS MANAGER

- Plan, research, and execute advertising and promotions to maintain good public image

- Choose events to enhance public image

- Promote company or athlete point of view

BROADCASTING

BASIC DEGREES AND SKILLS

- Audio-visual or media skills

- Writing skills

- Public speaking skills or drama background

- Foreign languages

- Bachelor's degree or experience with broadcast technology, electronics, or engineering

- Computer skills

COMMENTATOR AND REPORTER

- Collect information, study and organize news stories, and present information on the air
- Write opinions on news and events

BROADCASTING MANAGER

- Coordinate all radio and television activities
- Sometimes see to accounting, purchasing, hiring, and other office duties

SALES

- Sell ad time to sponsors, advertising agencies, and other buyers
- Study size and characteristics of potential audience

SPORTS FACILITY AND VENUE MARKETING

BASIC DEGREES AND SKILLS

- Bachelor's degree in business administration or liberal arts

- Master's or doctoral degree a plus

- Familiarity with marketing and business

- Public speaking skills

- Leadership skills

TICKET SALES

- Sell tickets

- Manage cash

- Inventory management

VENUE MANAGER

- Market venue as a whole

- Business management, event booking, fund-raising, and public outreach

FACILITY EXECUTIVE

- Advertising, promotions, marketing, and sales

- Public relations

SPORTS EVENT MANAGEMENT AND OPERATIONS MARKETING

BASIC DEGREES AND SKILLS

- Sports and event management degree

- Hospitality degree

- Experience or courses in marketing, economics, accounting, and business

- Computer skills

- Writing and communication skills

EVENT MANAGER

- Work with managers in advertising and promotions department to market event

- Forecast public interest in potential events

SPECIAL EVENTS COORDINATOR

- Market smaller events at a venue

- Research, design, plan, and coordinate special events

PRODUCT DEMONSTRATOR

- Hand out product samples to potential customers

- Demonstrate sample products

SIGNIFICANT POINTS

- Keen competition is expected for these highly coveted jobs.

- College graduates with related experience, a high level of creativity, and strong communication and computer skills should have the best job opportunities.

- High earnings, substantial travel, and long hours, including evenings and weekends, are common.

- Because of the importance and high visibility of their jobs, these managers are often prime candidates for advancement to the highest ranks.

NATURE OF THE WORK

Advertising, marketing, promotions, public relations, and sales managers coordinate their companies' market research, marketing strategy, sales, advertising, promotions, pricing, product development, and public relations activities. In small firms, the owner or chief executive officer might assume all advertising, promotions, marketing, sales, and public relations responsibilities. In large firms, which may offer numerous products and services nationally or even worldwide, an executive vice president directs overall advertising, marketing, promotions, sales, and public relations policies.

TRAINING, OTHER QUALIFICATIONS, AND ADVANCEMENT

A wide range of educational backgrounds is suitable for entry into advertising, marketing, promotions, public relations, and sales manager jobs, but many employers prefer college graduates with experience in related occupations.

EDUCATION AND TRAINING

For marketing, sales, and promotions management positions, employers often prefer a bachelor's or master's degree in business administration with an emphasis on marketing. Courses in business law, management, economics, accounting, finance, mathematics, and statistics are advantageous. In addition, the completion of an internship while the candidate is in school is highly recommended. In highly technical industries, such as computer and electronics manufacturing, a bachelor's degree in engineering or science, combined with a master's degree in business administration, is preferred.

For advertising management positions, some employers prefer a bachelor's degree in advertising or journalism. A relevant course of study might include classes in marketing, consumer behavior, market research, sales, communication methods and technology, visual arts, art history, and photography.

For public relations management positions, some employers prefer a bachelor's or master's degree in public relations or journalism. The applicant's curriculum should include courses in advertising, business administration, public affairs, public speaking, political science, and creative and technical writing.

Most advertising, marketing, promotions, public relations, and sales management positions are filled through promotions of experienced staff or related professional personnel. For example, many managers are former sales representatives; purchasing agents; buyers; or product, advertising, promotions, or public relations specialists. In small firms, in which the number of positions is limited, advancement to a management position usually comes slowly. In large firms, promotion may occur more quickly.

OTHER QUALIFICATIONS

Computer skills are necessary for record keeping and data management, and the ability to work in an Internet environment is becoming increasingly vital as more marketing, product promotion, and advertising is done through the Internet. Also, the ability to communicate in a foreign language may open up employment opportunities in many rapidly growing areas around the country, especially cities with large Spanish-speaking populations.

Persons interested in becoming advertising, marketing, promotions, public relations, and sales managers should be mature, creative, highly motivated, resistant to stress, flexible, and decisive. The ability to communicate persuasively, both orally and in writing, with other managers, staff, and the public is vital. These managers also need tact, good judgment, and an exceptional ability to establish and maintain effective personal relationships with supervisory and professional staff members and client firms.

CERTIFICATION AND ADVANCEMENT

Some associations offer certification programs for these managers. Certification—an indication of competence and achievement—is particularly important in a competitive job market. Although relatively few advertising, marketing, promotions, public relations, and sales managers currently are certified, the number of managers who seek certification is expected to grow. Today, there are numerous management certification programs based on education and job performance. In addition, the Public

Relations Society of America offers a certification program for public relations practitioners that is based on years of experience and performance on an examination.

Although experience, ability, and leadership are emphasized for promotion, advancement can be accelerated by participation in management training programs conducted by larger firms. Many firms also provide their employees with continuing education opportunities— either in-house or at local colleges and universities—and encourage employee participation in seminars and conferences, often held by professional societies. In collaboration with colleges and universities, numerous marketing and related associations sponsor national or local management training programs. Course subjects include brand and product management; international marketing; sales management evaluation; telemarketing and direct sales; interactive marketing; product promotion; marketing communication; market research; organizational communication; and data-processing systems, procedures, and management. Many firms pay all or part of the cost for employees who complete courses.

Because of the importance and high visibility of their jobs, advertising, marketing, promotions, public relations, and sales managers are often prime candidates for advancement to the highest ranks. Well-trained, experienced, and successful managers may be promoted to higher positions in their own or another firm; some become top executives.

Managers with extensive experience and sufficient capital may open their own businesses.

JOB OUTLOOK

Employment is projected to grow about as fast as average. As with most managerial jobs, keen competition is expected for these highly coveted positions.

EMPLOYMENT CHANGE

Overall employment of advertising, marketing, promotions, public relations, and sales managers is expected to increase by 13 percent through 2018. Job growth will be spurred by competition for a growing number of goods and services, both foreign and domestic, and the need to make one's product or service stand out in the crowd. In addition, as the influence of traditional advertising in newspapers, radio, and network television wanes, marketing professionals are being asked to develop new and different ways to advertise and promote products and services to better reach potential customers.

Sales and marketing managers and their departments constitute some of the most important personnel in an organization and are less subject to downsizing or outsourcing than are other types of managers, except in the case of companies that are consolidating. Employment of these managers, therefore, will vary primarily on the basis of the growth or contraction in the industries that employ them. Employment of marketing managers will grow about as fast as average at 12 percent between 2008 and 2018, and that of sales managers will grow faster than average at 15 percent over the same period.

Advertising and promotions managers are expected to experience little or no change in employment from 2008 to 2018. Despite large declines in the number of advertising managers in recent years, due mainly to the sharp reduction in the number of advertising agencies and newspaper and periodical publishers, which employ the greatest numbers of these managers, advertising and promotions managers are not expected to experience similar declines in the future. Because advertising is the primary source of revenue for most media, advertising departments are less affected in a downturn. An expected increase in the number of television and radio stations and a sharp increase in the amount of advertising in digital media, such as the Internet and wireless devices, will generate a need for advertising managers to oversee new and innovative advertising programs. A number of these advertising managers will be self-employed.

Public relations managers are expected to see an increase in employment of 13 percent between 2008 and 2018, which is about as fast as average for all occupations, as organizations increasingly emphasize community outreach and customer relations as a way to enhance their reputation and visibility. Especially among the growing number of nonprofit organizations, such as education services, business and professional associations, and hospitals, where many of these workers are employed, public relations managers will be charged with promoting the mission of the organization and encouraging membership or use of the organization's services.

JOB PROSPECTS

Most job openings for this occupation will be due to the need to replace workers who leave the occupation or retire. However, advertising, marketing, promotions, public relations, and sales manager jobs are highly coveted and are often sought by other managers or highly experienced professionals, resulting in keen competition. College graduates with related experience, a high level of creativity, and strong communication and computer skills should have the best job opportunities. In particular, employers will seek those who have the skills to conduct new types of advertising, marketing, promotions, public relations, and sales campaigns involving new media, particularly the Internet.

WORK ENVIRONMENT

Advertising, marketing, promotions, public relations, and sales managers work in offices close to those of top managers. Working under pressure is unavoidable when schedules change and problems arise, but deadlines and goals still must be met.

Substantial travel may be required in order to meet with customers and consult with others in the industry. Sales managers travel to national, regional, and local offices and to the offices of various dealers and distributors. Advertising and promotions managers may travel to meet with clients or representatives of communications media. At times, public relations managers travel to meet with special-interest groups or government officials. Job transfers between headquarters and regional offices are common, particularly among sales managers.

Long hours, including evenings and weekends are common. In 2008, over 80 percent of advertising, marketing, promotions, public relations, and sales managers worked 40 hours or more a week.

GLOSSARY

accredited Officially accepted or certified.

advocate To support the cause of another.

amateur Someone who takes part in sports or other activity recreationally, but not as a profession.

app Short for "application," a program that runs on a cell phone or other mobile device, like a smartphone.

brainstorm The act of formulating new ideas (sometimes as a group) to solve a problem or make a plan.

buyer Someone who obtains ownership, possession, or rights to the use or services of something, usually through payment.

closed-circuit television A signal that is only broadcast to a limited group of people.

cold calling The act of contacting a business or individual without any previous introduction or common connections, usually to initiate the sale of a product or service.

commercial Describing anything that is undertaken for profit.

concession stand A booth that sells refreshments like drinks and snacks at a stadium or other venue.

continuing education Formal education usually for adult students on a part-time basis.

corporate event An association or business event.

damage control Actions taken to reduce harm to a company or person's character after a negative action or comment.

endorsement Recommending a product, usually for money.

entrepreneur Someone in charge of managing or organizing a business or project who usually takes on all the risks.

ethical Conforming to approved traditional values or behavior.

executive An upper-level employee who has supervisory or organizational responsibilities.

forecast To predict results.

incentive A factor, often a reward or bonus, that encourages or motivates one to act.

inventory The stockpile of goods on hand.

kinesiology Principles of mechanics and anatomy in relation to human movement.

microblogging Short-form blog posting designed for speed and efficiency through technologies such as Twitter.

personnel A group of people usually employed by a company.

press release Information released to the media about an event.

profit Income after all expenses.

promotion Sale of goods, usually by offering a discount.

revenue Income from an event, sale of a product, or other resource.

scholarship A grant of money given to a student to follow a course of study.

shareholder Someone who owns part, or a share, of stock in a company.

slogan A short phrase used in advertising and promotions to grab a consumer's attention.

smartphone A computerized, high-end mobile phone that has far more networking functions than a telephone.

spin To emphasize a certain interpretation of something to sway opinion.

sponsor A person, group, or company that pays for or organizes an event, often to have its name associated with that activity.

tie-in Something that relates (ties in) or connects to a promotion.

tuition The price paid for educational training.

venue A place or location where certain kinds of events are held.

VIP (very important person) Usually a powerful individual or high-ranking official that is given special treatment.

wholesale Referring to the selling of products, usually in a large amount, for resale.

FOR MORE INFORMATION

American Management Association
1601 Broadway
New York, NY 10019
(877) 566-9441
Web site: http://www.amanet.org
The American Management Association is a nonprofit organization that enables individuals, companies, and organizations to search for management jobs, view training seminars and Webcasts, and catch up on the latest news in management.

American Marketing Association (AMA)
311 S. Wacker Drive, Suite 5800
Chicago, IL 60606
(800) AMA-1150 (262-1150)
Web site: http://www.marketingpower.com
The AMA is the professional association for individuals and organizations who are leading the practice, teaching, and development of marketing worldwide.

Canadian Management Centre

150 York Street, Suite 500

Toronto, ON M5H 3S5

Canada

(416) 214-5678

Web site: http://www.cmctraining.org

The Canadian Management Centre provides professional development and management training programs in Canada, including training courses in communications, customer service, purchasing, and marketing sales.

Canadian Marketing Association

1 Concorde Gate, Suite 607

Don Mills, ON M3C 3N6

Canada

(416) 391-2362

Web site: http://www.the-cma.org

The Canadian Marketing Association (CMA) offers programs that help shape the future of marketing in Canada by building talented marketers and exceptional business leaders and by demonstrating marketing's strategic role as a key driver of business success.

Department of Sport and Entertainment Management

University of South Carolina

Carolina Coliseum, Room 2012

Columbia, SC 29208

(803) 777-4690

Web site: http://www.sportandentertainment.org

The Sport and Entertainment Management Department at the University of South Carolina prepares undergraduate and graduate students for a variety of positions in the sports and entertainment industry.

International Special Events Society

401 N. Michigan Avenue

Chicago, IL 60611-4267

(800) 688-4737

Web site: http://www.ises.com

The International Special Events Society offers event professionals the latest news, provides a forum for community, and encourages high standards in business practices.

North American Society for Sport Management

NASSM Business Office

135 Winterwood Drive

Butler, PA 16001

(724) 482-6277

Web site: http://www.nassm.com

The North American Society for Sport Management supports and helps professionals in sports, leisure, and recreation to promote, stimulate, and encourage study, research, scholarly writing, and professional development in the area of sport management.

The Public Relations Society of America (PRSA)
33 Maiden Lane, 11th Floor
New York, NY 10038-5150
(212) 460-1400
Web site: http://www.prsa.org
The PRSA is the nation's largest community of public relations and communications professionals. It provides training and advocates for a greater understanding and adoption of public relations services.

WEB SITES

Due to the changing nature of Internet links, Rosen Publishing has developed an online list of Web sites related to the subject of this book. This site is updated regularly. Please use this link to access the list:

http://www.rosenlinks.com/gcsi/mark

FOR FURTHER READING

Ali, Moi. *Public Relations: Creating an Image* (Influence and Persuasion). Chicago, IL: Heinemann-Raintree, 2005.

Cotts, David G., Kathy O. Roper, and Richard P. Payant. *The Facility Management Handbook.* 3rd ed. New York, NY: AMACOM, 2009.

Davis, John. *The Olympic Games Effect: How Sports Marketing Builds Strong Brands.* Hoboken, NJ: John Wiley & Sons, 2008.

Dawson, Matt. *Sponsored Life: The Ultimate Guide to Skateboarding Sponsorship.* San Juan Capistrano, CA: Luma Publications, 2008.

Favorito, Joseph. *Sports Publicity: A Practical Approach.* Burlington, MA: Elsevier Ltd., 2007.

Ferguson Publishing Company. *Broadcasting (Careers in Focus).* 3rd ed. New York, NY: Ferguson Publishing Company, 2007.

Hawk, Tony, and Pat Hawk. *How Did I Get Here? The Ascent of an Unlikely CEO.* Hoboken, NJ: John Wiley & Sons, 2010.

Hayden, C. J. *Get Clients Now: A 28-Day Marketing Program for Professionals, Consultants, and Coaches.* New York, NY: AMACOM, 2007.

Heitzmann, Ray. *Careers for Sports Nuts & Other Athletic Types.* 3rd ed. New York, NY: McGraw-Hill, 2004.

Hopwood, Maria, James Skinner, and Paul Kitchin. *Sport Public Relations and Communication.* Burlington, MA: Elsevier Ltd., 2010.

Irwin, Richard, William Sutton, and Larry McCarthy.

Sport Promotion and Sales Management. 2nd ed.
Champaign, IL: Human Kinetics, 2008.

Morgan, Melissa Johnson, and Jane Summers. *Sports Marketing.* Victoria, Australia: Cengage Learning Australia, 2005

Mullin, Bernard, Stephen Hardy, and William Suttun. *Sport Promotion and Sales Management.* 3rd ed. Champaign, IL: Human Kinetics, 2007.

Pitts, Brenda G. and David K. Stotlar. *Fundamentals of Sport Marketing.* 3rd ed. Morgantown, WV: Fitness Information Technology, 2002.

Rein, Irving, Philip Kotler, and Ben Shields. *The Elusive Fan: Reinventing Sports in a Crowded Marketplace.* New York, NY: McGraw-Hill, 2006.

Rovell, Darren. *First in Thirst: How Gatorade Turned the Science of Sweat into a Cultural Phenomenon.* New York, NY: AMACOM, 2006.

Shilbury, David, Hans Westerbeek, and Shayne Quick. *Strategic Sport Marketing.* 2nd ed. Crows Nest, Australia: Allen & Unwin, 2003.

Spoelstra, Jon. *Marketing Outrageously Redux: How to Increase Your Revenue by Staggering Amounts.* Rev. ed. Austin, TX: Bard Press, 2010.

Stotlar, David K. *Developing Successful Sport Marketing Plans.* Morgantown, WV: Fitness Information Technology, 2009.

Swados, Robert O. *Counsel in the Crease: A Big League Player in the Hockey Wars.* Amherst, NY: Prometheus Books, 2006.

Tymorek, Stan. *Advertising & Marketing.* New York, NY: Ferguson Publishing Company, 2010.

Unger, Harlow G. *But What If I Don't Want to Go to College?* 3rd ed. New York, NY: Ferguson Publishing Company, 2006.

BIBLIOGRAPHY

Bevilaqua, John P. "What Exactly Is Sports Marketing?" The Sport Digest. Retrieved August 20, 2011 (http://thesportdigest.com/archive/article/just-exactly-what-sports-marketing).

Bureau of Labor Statistics, U.S. Department of Labor. Retrieved August 21, 2011 (http://www.bls.gov/oco/ocos020.htm).

Dahl, Sima. "Networking 101." Retrieved August 21, 2011(http://www.marketingpower.com/Careers/Documents/Networking101.pdf).

Esposito, Anthony (director of ticket operations, Atlanta Braves). Interview with the author, July 22, 2011, and August 3, 2011.

Ewing, Jack. "Sports Sponsorship: A Risky Game." *Businessweek*. Retrieved July 28, 2011 (http://www.businessweek.com/globalbiz/content/jun2007/gb20070607_140258.htm).

Graham, Stedman, Lisa Delpy Meirotti, and Joe Jeff Goldblatt. *The Ultimate Guide to Sports Marketing*. 2nd ed. New York, NY: McGraw-Hill, 2001.

Hawk, Tony, and Pat Hawk. *How Did I Get Here? The Ascent of an Unlikely CEO*. Hoboken, NJ: John Wiley and Sons, 2010.

Heitner, Darren (Dynasty Athlete Representation). Interview with the author, July 8, 2011.

Helitzer, Melvin. *The Dream Job: Sports Publicity, Promotion and Marketing*. 3rd ed. Athens, OH: University Sports Press, 2000.

Hofmann Stephanie (head of agency development, IPG, Google, Inc.; former vice president of marketing for the WNBA). Interview with the author, July 26, 2011.

Kaser, Ken, and Dotty B. Oelkers. *Sports and Entertainment Marketing*. 2nd ed. Mason, OH: Thompson South-Western, 2005. Retrieved August 21, 2011 (http://websites.swlearning.com/cgi-wadsworth/course_products_wp.pl?fid=M20b&product_isbn_issn=0538438894&disciplene_number=415).

Layton, Julia. "What Exactly Does a Boxing Promoter Do?" Retrieved August 17, 2011 (http://entertain-ment.howstuffworks.com/boxing-promoter.htm).

Lee, Johnny K. "Marketing and Promotion of the Olympic Games." *Sports Journal*, vol. 8, no. 3, 2005. Retrieved July 27, 2011 (http://www.thesportjournal.org/article/marketing-and-promotion-olympic-games).

Schaaf, Phil. *Sports Marketing: It's Not Just a Game Anymore*. Amherst, NY: Prometheus Books, 1995.

Tuchman, Robert. "Taking Sports Marketing from Passion to Pocketbook." Retrieved August 20, 2011 (http://www.entrepreneur.com/startingabusiness/youngentrepreneurs/columnistroberttuchman/article205912.html).

USA Today. "3 Olympians Get Wheaties Boxes, Not Just Gold Medals." Retrieved August 20, 2011 (http://www.usatoday.com/money/advertising/2004-09-01-wheaties_x.htm).

(http://www.usatoday.com/money/advertising/2004-09-01-wheaties_x.htm).

Vomhof, John, Jr. "Target Field Named Sports Facility of the Year." *Minneapolis/St. Paul Business Journal*, May 19, 2011. Retrieved August 19, 2011 (http://www.bizjournals.com/twincities/blog/sports-busi-ness/2011/05/target-field-named-sports-facility-of.html).

INDEX

ABOUT THE AUTHOR

Heather Moore Niver is a New York State author, editor, and poet. She has participated in juried writing workshops at the New York State Writer's Institute and the Edna St. Vincent Millay Society, and every winter she leads a writing workshop at an Adirondack arts retreat. She has written other books about sports cars, the nervous system, and animals.

PHOTO CREDITS

Cover, p. 1 © www.istockphoto.com/jacomstephens; cover background, pp. 20, 78–79 Shutterstock.com; p. 4 DVM Sports; p. 10 Daniel Acker/Bloomberg via Getty Images; p. 12 Bill Hogan/Chicago Tribune/McClatchy-Tribune/Getty Images; p. 17 George Gojkovich/Getty Images; p. 24 Justin Sullivan/Getty Images; p. 27 © www.istockphoto.com/hidesy; p. 28 © www.istockphoto.com/monkeybusinessimages; p. 32 STR/AFP/Getty Images; p. 34 Jamie Squire/Getty Images; pp. 38–39 Joe Murphy/NBAE/Getty Images; p. 43 AFP/Getty Images; p. 46 © Michelle D. Bidwell/PhotoEdit; p. 48 ©TriStar Pictures/courtesy Everett Collection; p. 52 © www.istockphoto.com/damircudic; p. 56 Adrian Dennis/AFP/Getty Images; p. 59 © www.istockphoto.com/andearoad; p. 60 Michael C. Weimar/The New York Times/ Redux; p. 63 John P. Filo/CBS/Landov; p. 67 © www.istockphoto.com/track5; p. 68 Mat Szwajkos/Getty Images; p. 70 George Doyle/Stockbyte/Thinkstock; p. 75 aceshit1/Shutterstock.com; pp. 85, 87 © AP Images; pp. 90–91 Juan Camilo Bernal/Shutterstock.com; interior design elements: © www.istockphoto.com/hudiemm (grid pattern); http://lostandtaken.com (striped border); pp. 8, 19, 31, 42, 51, 62, 73, 82, 93, 95, 102, 111, 114, 118, 120, 123 (montage) © www.istockphoto.com, Shutterstock.com

Designer: Brian Garvey; Editor: Nicholas Croce;
Photo Researcher: Marty Levick